Dear Max & Lukey,   Jan 2015

Here are a few things to look
out for when you come
and visit...
We can't wait to see you!!

Lots of love,

        Uncle Josh, Aunty Eva,

        Ben, Noah and Mya
                                    xxx

FOR TANGUY TÉO & CHARLOTTE

For Ivy and Moss; Lily, Nina and Bibi;
and for Phillip.

ALPHABETICAL SYDNEY

ANTONIA PESENTI & HILARY BELL

NEWSOUTH

This is our Sydney. We'll show you the sights

From Allawah over to Bonnyrigg Heights,

Through Cattai to Dee Why and on to East Ryde,

Past Five Dock and Glebe, Hurlstone Park, Ingleside,

Jannali, Killara, Lane Cove, Manly Vale,

A swim at North Curl Curl, then south to Oakdale.

There's Potts Point and Queenscliff, Rose Bay, Summer Hill;

See Tempe and Ultimo, see Varroville;

Then Woolloomooloo for a pie by the water,

And west to Yagoona (by Strathfield – it's shorter),

Back down through Kurnell, where you visit the wetland,

Take Anzac Parade and you end up in Zetland.

What happened to **X**?

We must not leave a gap!

Perhaps **X** marks the spot?

So now get out your map …

A's for **amusement park**: step right this way!

Shrieks of delight over Lavender Bay,

'Welcome,' it cries, with its lunatic grin,

'Welcome to Sydney! Now won't you come in?'

B is for **bats**, who sojourn after dark

To the Gardens across from Centennial Park.

They squeal until sunrise, then back they commute

To hang from the palm trees like stinky black fruit.

C's for **cicadas**. They hatch underground,

But once out, they make the most deafening sound.

Look for their see-through brown shells, which they leave

For you to stick onto your friend's jumper sleeve.

The **D**elicatessen is our corner shop.

Want some mixed lollies? Sunglasses? A mop?

A fridge hums with olives – black, oily and glossy –

And feta and cheddar and red cabanossi.

April brings with it the Royal **E**aster Show:

Prize-winning pumpkins, the wild rodeo,

Toddlers in Teacups with saucer-wide eyes,

Codgers in Dodgems with stodgy meat pies.

N WAY CANTEEN EAT

ASTY MEAT PIES

TAIRY FLOSS

LAUGHING CLOWNS

A PRIZE EVERY TIME

SHOWBAGS

PRIZEWINNING
CAKES JAMS CHUTNEYS

CHAMPION

GRAND CHAMPION

RESERVE CHAMPION

$5 PER RIDE

TICKETS

Sweet **F**rangipanis – their summery scent,

Rubbery leaves and their branches all bent;

Falling on footpaths and filling the gutter,

White as vanilla and yellow as butter.

GARAGE SALE

today!!

23 AUGUST From 9·30 AM!!

AVOCA STREET

RANDWICK

EVERYTHING MUST GO!!

MONOPOLY

G is for **garage sales**, every weekend:

Clocks, frocks, an Xbox in need of a mend,

Bicycles, board games, a lone rollerblade,

And if you're lucky, some cold lemonade!

: Harbour Bridge, where the traffic is bound

North to the south, and the other way round.

Walk it and climb it, drive over and under;

Stand right beneath and the trains are like thunder.

SYDNEY HARBOUR TUNNEL

LOW CLEARANCE

I is for **ibis**. Just look how she fishes

In rubbish bins looking for something delicious.

Their beaks long and curving, and snappy as pegs;

Grimy white feathers and scaly black legs.

J is for Sydney's two favourite flowers,

Neither is native, but both we call ours.

Drop, **jacaranda**, your soft lilac rain;

Jasmine, climb fences in every back lane.

Big boxy head and a flash of blue wing:

Here's **K**ookaburra, our merry Bush King.

One clever eye on the lizard he's after …

Smelling a storm, he erupts into laughter.

L is for **lawn bowls**, all red brick and ants,

White shoes and hats, a crisp crease in the pants.

Bend at the knee, and send your ball over

The sunbaked flat grass, closely weeded of clover.

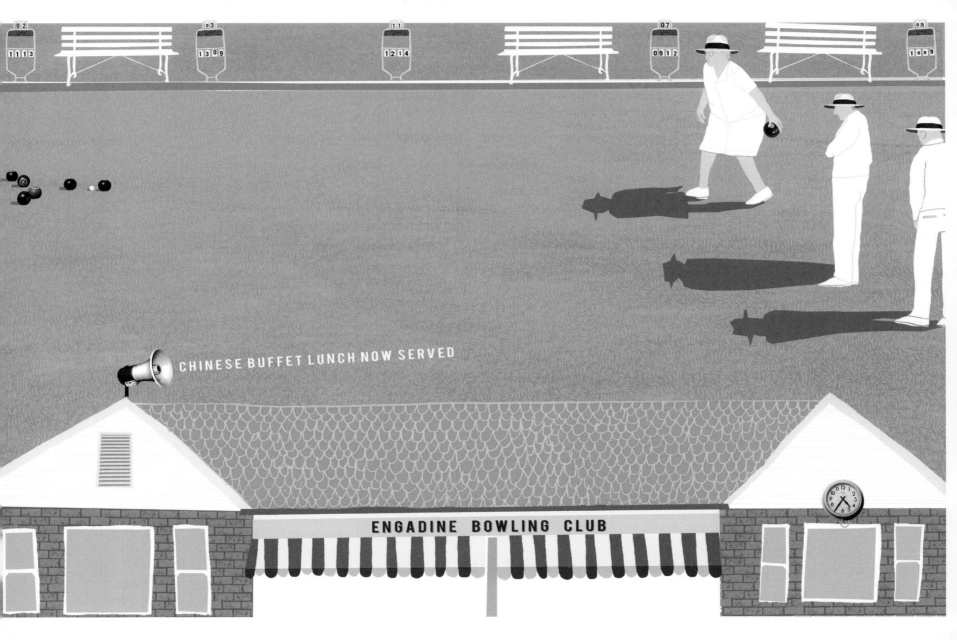

M is for **Moreton Bay fig**, standing tall.

See how his roots twist and tangle and sprawl.

Down tumble tiny brown figs when it blows,

Seedy and squashy, get stuck in your toes.

is for **nature strip**, jewel of the 'burb,

Two feet of grass between footpath and kerb.

Garbage night: roll out your red wheelie bin –

But watch out for bindis, they're sharp as a pin!

What do you dream of while dozing at school?

Diving down deep in a green Ocean pool.

Swim with the mermaids in pink bathing caps,

Wrinkled and leathery, doing their laps.

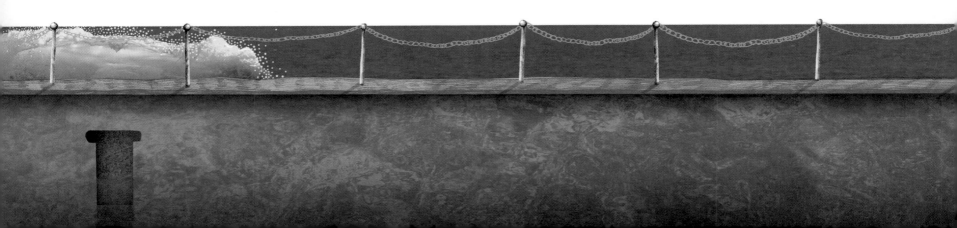

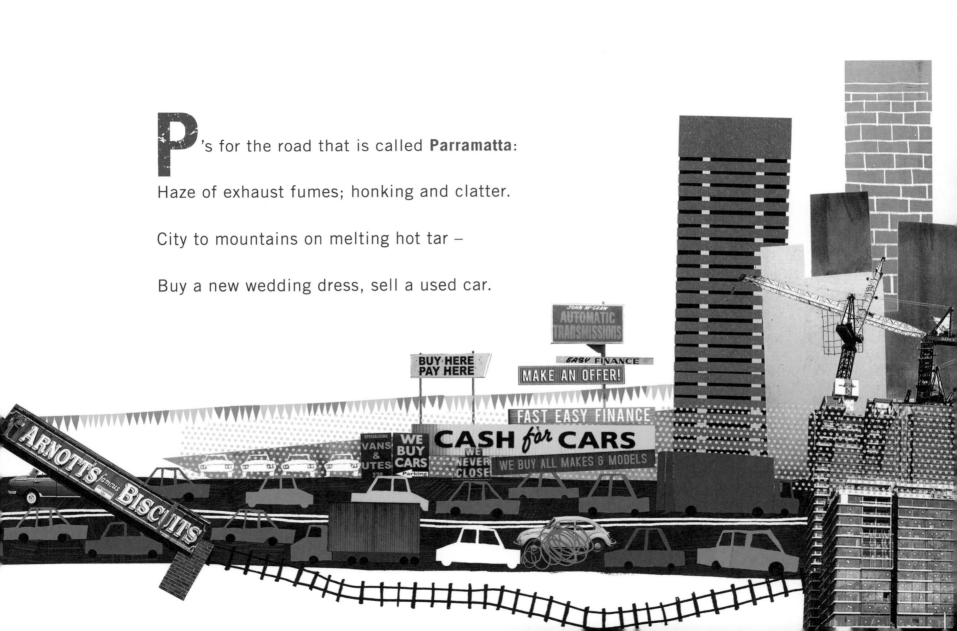

P 's for the road that is called **Parramatta**:

Haze of exhaust fumes; honking and clatter.

City to mountains on melting hot tar –

Buy a new wedding dress, sell a used car.

Circular **Q**uay, full of ferries and ships,

Glittering harbour and greasy hot chips,

Pigeons and didge-players (visitors love them),

Cars, trains and buses all stacked up above them.

R: renovations – the clanging and clamouring,

Ladders and scaffolding, banging and hammering.

Here comes the pool and the pond full of fish,

The ensuite, the guest wing, the satellite dish!

S is for sundress and sunhat and sun,

But here it's for **sunburn**, which isn't much fun.

Now we wear rashies, but once, red as crabs,

We'd peel off the skin and then pick at the scabs!

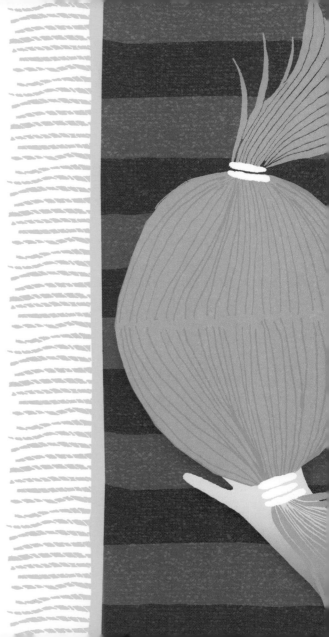

Terraces running in rows up our streets.

Wrought-iron balconies, drying the sheets.

Gracious old houses, all matching but not:

One's poky, one's paved, one has pinks in a pot.

After a stifling hot day, storm clouds muster,

Soon there's a gust of a southerly buster

Slamming the screen door and rattling the pane.

U for **umbrellas!** as down comes the rain.

A swim in the sea can be lovely, but what'll

You do if you're stung by an angry bluebottle?

Vinegar used to be splashed onto nips;

These days we keep it for hot fish'n'chips.

A summery tune and a bad-tempered man ...

Let's run, Mr **W**hippy is stopping his van!

Choc-tops with nuts or with sprinkles and Flakes,

Pink ice-cream cones and Blue Heaven milkshakes.

X for **Xpress bus**, the one that we took

When we **xplored** all the things in this book.

Hop on before it goes rumbling past,

An **xcellent** way to see Sydney – and fast.

Shout 'yum' for **Y**um Cha! It's heaven on wheels:

Scrumptious prawn dumplings, gelatinous eels,

Gow gee and green tea, fried oysters, spilt soy,

For Saturday breakfast, or *Kung Hei Fat Choi*!*

(* Chinese New Year greeting)

Let's linger in Sydney a little bit longer:

Z is for zoo, our beloved Taronga.

Wallabies, tree snakes, a sweet dromedary;

Hooray for the seals, and then home on the ferry.

Antonia Pesenti is an award-winning architect and illustrator whose work has appeared in magazines around the world. She loves cities, and she loves to draw: creating *Alphabetical Sydney* was her dream project.

Hilary Bell is a playwright whose plays have been produced in Australia and overseas, including by the Sydney Theatre Company and Steppenwolf in the US. She has won an Aurealis Award for young adult fiction. Her favourite pastime is walking Sydney's back lanes and secret steps, muttering four-line verses to herself.

A NewSouth book

Published by
NewSouth Publishing
University of New South Wales Press Ltd
University of New South Wales
Sydney NSW 2052
AUSTRALIA

newsouthpublishing.com

© Antonia Pesenti and Hilary Bell 2013
First published 2013

10 9 8 7 6

ISBN 9781742233703

A Cataloguing-in-Publication entry is available from the National Library of Australia catalogue at www.nla.gov.au

Design Antonia Pesenti and Natalie Winter
Printer Everbest

This book is printed on paper using fibre supplied from plantation or sustainably managed forests.

UNSW
AUSTRALIA